Contents

GW00703032

STOCK

Introduction

Addison Wesley Longman has worked together with the Economics and Business Education Association (EBEA) on this series in order to provide material for the numerate parts of Business Studies courses. As these are sections which students often find difficult, it is important to create an interesting, accessible approach.

The cause of much difficulty is that many students lack confidence in their own ability to work with numbers and therefore underperform in exams. One objective of the books, therefore, is to help build confidence and provide students with a strategy which enables them first to understand and then to put the ideas into practice.

Each topic is introduced through a practical explanation using a straightforward, realistic example. It is then developed by providing material for the student to work on and suggestions for further work. The introductory example will also provide a resource for students when working on other material as it provides a model to work from. The book is therefore a handy revision aid. The series is designed to meet the needs of all exam boards.

The introduction of Key Skills provides a wealth of opportunity for Business Studies courses. Few subjects are in such a strong position to develop students' abilities in these fields. As Key Skills become an integral part of programmes from Key Stage 1 to A-level, students will be seeking ways of building a portfolio of work across the subjects.

Each book in this series has been written by a group of practising teachers who have come together under the auspices of the EBEA. They have worked as a team to identify the needs of students and create materials which are aimed at helping to build expertise. This strategy ensures that the material is practical, relevant and appropriate for students.

The EBEA can be contacted at 1a Keymer Road, Hassocks, East Sussex, BN8 8AD; tel. 01273 846033; e-mail address, ebeah@pavilion.co.uk.

Taking stock

In this section you will:

▶ draw and interpret a stock control diagram,

▶ identify the key issues involved in stock control,

▶ understand the significance of stock control when considering lean production.

Your task

A building company uses large quantities of sand and needs to ensure it has enough in stock at any time to meet the ups and downs of the building trade. It uses stock at a rate of 100 tonnes per month.

> What would be the costs of running the business with too little or too much stock? Draw a diagram to represent the pattern of stock movement that you might expect over a year.

Getting started

How do you think a building company would order the sand? How often would the order arrive? Where would it be kept until use? What else might space in a building yard be used for? When will the sand have to be paid for? What kind of cash flow problems might arise?

You could think about a diagram with months on one axis and quantities of sand delivered and used on the other axis. How quickly might stocks be used? Would this vary between summer and winter?

Over the past two or three decades, following the lead of the Japanese, in particular the car company Toyota, the control of stock has become a significant issue in the drive to reduce costs, make production more flexible and suppliers more reliable.

When a business considers the level of stock it needs to hold, it will consider all those factors which will mean extra costs as the level of stock rises. Briefly, these will comprise:
- space available for storage, insurance, chance of theft, chance of stock becoming obsolete (especially relevant if the business sells technologically advanced products),
- chance of stock deterioration (relevant to a food producer), organising the receipt and placement of stock, finance costs and opportunity costs.

Finance costs deserve an extra note – it is likely that a business will have to pay for its stock before it gets the money in from sales of the stock. This is usually done by arranging an overdraft with the bank, and this incurs an interest penalty. If the company held an average of £50 000 in stock and paid an interest charge of 10%, the cost of financing this level of stock would be
$$10\% \times £50\,000 = £5000.$$

These must be balanced by those costs which will <u>decrease</u> as the level of stock rises:
- costs per unit due to purchasing economies of scale,
- costs of a stock-out (running out of stock) in terms of lost sales.

The pattern of stock movement could be shown in a diagram as on page 3.

It assumes the business receives stock of 300 tonnes of sand every three months, but has to order one month in advance because of the unreliability of the supplier. It also likes to hold a <u>buffer</u> stock of 50 tonnes, just in case the supplier is late! It uses the stock at a rate of 100 tonnes per month.

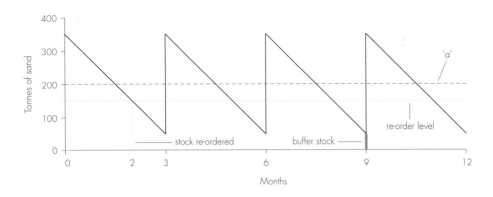

Evaluating the data

What assumptions does this diagram make about the way stocks are used? How else does this model simplify real business practice?

Several points are worth noting from the diagram above. The straight diagonal lines indicate that stock is used <u>constantly</u> at a rate of 300 tonnes per month; hardly the case in real life! It is also assumed that suppliers deliver on time and that all of the stock is of the right standard for use. This means the buffer stock is not used. Given these rather broad assumptions, we can use the diagram for further analysis.

What does this diagram suggest about the average level of stock?

How might the company go about reducing the level of stock if it proves too costly to maintain at present levels?

The average level of stock is represented by line 'a' which goes through the mid-point of the diagonal and is calculated by maximum stock + minimum stock ÷ 2, i.e. the average of the two. This will give us a value of (350 + 50) ÷ 2 = 200 tonnes.

If, for example, each tonne costs £80, then the average amount of money tied up in stock is 200 × £80 = £16 000. Applying an interest rate of 10% gives a finance cost of £1600 per annum. We can also conclude that stock <u>turns over</u> 4 times a year.

If the business decides that the cost of holding all these tonnes of sand is too much, how does it go about reducing it?

Firstly, it must arrange with the suppliers to deliver a smaller amount, but more frequently. Then it must arrange for the more frequent deliveries to be received, which will presumably increase the administration costs. The sand is likely to be stored in the same place, but initially more of the space will be unused, which is inefficient. The company may also lose any bulk purchase discounts, although it will be ordering the same amount and close negotiation with the supplier will probably mean it maintains the discount.

Overall, there does not seem to be any short-term advantage of holding less stock although in the longer term the business ought to save money. Supposing we move to a delivery of 12 times per year, keeping the same buffer stock. This would mean stock turns over 12 times a year and the average amount held is reduced.

Draw a diagram to represent this means of stock control, and assess where the benefits lie.

Going further

You are a supplier to Toyota cars, one of Japan's largest car producers. Toyota have decided to cut the stocks they carry to the lowest possible levels. What might be the consequences for your business?

By holding less stock, the business will have less money tied up in working capital, which means it can be released into the business for other uses. Money is released only when stock is reduced and _not_ replaced.

In the earlier example, at month 9 the business would normally have replaced 300 tonnes of sand, but now it is only replacing 250; this is a one-off saving in cost meaning the money will stay in the business.

The arguments in favour of lower stock have pushed modern businesses to reduce their average stocks to the lowest possible level. This level, by definition, is at a point when the stock arrives just before it is needed; this is known as 'Just in Time'. Companies like Nissan have mastered this to a fine art – they have reduced the stock-holding time for the carpets of their cars to almost zero. The supplier only finds out it must cut the carpet when the car hits the assembly line!

In order for a business to be able to manage the process of JIT effectively, it must forge close and long-lasting links with its suppliers. Supply chain management, which looks closely at the work of suppliers to identify costs which could be cut, has become part of the process for any business using JIT. Supplying Toyota – one of the most famous companies in the world (it operates the most efficient and productive factory in the world at its base in Japan) is hard work. Toyota will dictate the prices and the penalties for late delivery, but in return will use their own expertise to identify potential cost savings within the supplier's operations and will award a long-term contract. The supplier is at the beck and call of Toyota; late deliveries are just not worth it! It has been known for lorry drivers to carry entire sets of replacement tyres, just in case there is a multiplicity of punctures.

JIT in Japan is slowly becoming unworkable as the traffic systems become more congested. The earthquake at Kobe grounded several factories almost immediately because the main highway crashed from its pillars. The alternative name for JIT has become 'Just in Trucks', as stock is held up in traffic jams!

One of the major issues which JIT raises is that with a much lower level of stock, sudden orders, machinery break-downs, absent workforce, late deliveries and poor quality will be spotted more frequently. In the past, with large levels of stock, any disruption to the production process could be cushioned with the levels of stock. By reducing the stock to its minimum the problems are revealed and solved, thereby increasing quality, reliability of machines and suppliers, as well as relying much more on employees to do their job right first time.

Extension tasks

A business orders products to be delivered every 2 months. Each delivery is for 1000 units and the buffer stock is 100 units.

How much stock is used per month ? What is the average level of stock? Use a diagram to help you.

How would the answers to these two questions alter if
(a) delivery was made every month?
(b) the buffer was reduced to 50 units?
(c) delivery was increased to 1200 units per month?
(d) all three of the above were implemented?

You will need to re-draw the diagram each time.

Enterprise in action?

In this section you will:

▶ use a cash flow forecast to spot trends in income and expenditure,

▶ assess the impact of figures on a business,

▶ suggest suitable strategies for the business to adopt in the light of its cash flow situation.

Your task

A successful business needs to plan ahead, and this is especially true when it comes to handling money. It is important to keep track of the money going out of the business and the money coming in so that there will always be enough available to pay the regular bills and to buy whatever is needed. A cash flow forecast helps the business to do this and provides an opportunity to spot problems and sort them out before they become serious.

You and several of your friends decide to set up a Young Enterprise company. You plan to make wooden toys to sell at Christmas fairs and local craft outlets, but in order to raise some cash to buy stock, you decide to hold a disco. A Young Enterprise adviser, a member of staff at a local bank, is on hand to give you advice on the running of the company. Your adviser suggests you draw up a cash flow forecast to help you to predict what your costs and revenues might be.

Analyse the cash flow forecast and devise suitable strategies for the Young Enterprise company to follow. Then:

either as the company's adviser, write a letter to the managing director setting out your recommendations regarding the management of cash flow, explaining your reasoning and outlining the possible consequences if the company carries on regardless of your suggestions,

or as the financial director of the company, make a presentation to others in your company, using overhead transparencies to assist you, in which you outline the potential problems facing the company and explain what should be done to tackle them.

Datafile

Table 1

Young Enterprise company cash flow forecast

	Oct.	Nov.	Dec.	Jan.	Feb.	Mar.	Apr.
Income							
Shares	70						
Sales		30	625	0	50	50	50
Sponsorship							
Total	70	30	625	–	50	50	50
Expenditure							
Registration fee	65						
Wages	21	28	21	28	21	28	14
Hall booking fee	50						
Disco booking fee	90						
Decorations			25				
Refreshments			100				
Administration expenses	3	15	15	0	3	3	3
Wood		25					
Paint, fabric, etc.		15					
Packaging for toys		4					
Total	229	87	161	28	24	31	17
Net cash flow	−159	−57	464	−28	26	19	33
Opening balance	0	−159	−216	248	220	246	265
Closing balance	−159	−216	248	220	246	265	298

Getting started

First, you need to examine the data in the cash flow forecast shown in Table 1. In order to do this, it would be helpful to show some of the data in the form of a graph.

Plot a line graph with three separate lines to show the monthly income, the net cash flow and the closing bank balance. Use different coloured lines for each item.

Remember to allow for negative numbers when you draw the axes for your graph. (You could use a spreadsheet to plot the graph.)

Look carefully at the bottom three rows in the cash flow forecast. How are these figures calculated? What is the significance of the timing of the expenses and income?

Going further

On what assumptions is the cash flow forecast based?

In order to answer this, you need to consider how the financial director has come up with the figures in the cash flow forecast. For example, how has the income in December been calculated? What might affect this figure?

What happens to the closing bank balance if the timings of income and expense items change? For example, what effect would it have if the company could pay for the disco after the event instead of beforehand?

One way to do this is to key the data into a spreadsheet. Manipulate the large income and expense items to see if it is possible for the company to avoid a negative closing bank balance.

Drawing conclusions

Using the total income row from the cash flow forecast in Table 1, why was income so high in December? What trend can you see if you look at the income line?

Using the net cash flow row, what problem can you see?

Using the closing bank balance row, is the company in a better position at the end of the trading period than it was at the beginning?

Do you think that the company is profitable in spite of the negative cash flow? Is there any other information you would want to know in order to answer the question fully?

Is negative cash flow a problem? If so, why?

Is profitability important? If so, why?

If another, more popular, event staged the same night as the disco caused actual takings in December to be £300 less than anticipated, how would this affect the profitability and the cash flow?

Evaluating the data

From your understanding of the company's finances, what would your letter or presentation recommend that it should do?

Identify at least five ways in which cash flow problems experienced by small firms can be eased. Which of these methods would be useful to the Young Enterprise company?

If the company does not adopt an approach which minimises cash flow problems, then it might need to raise extra finance. Where could the company get it from? Try to identify more than one source and consider which would be the most appropriate for it to use.

Are there any marketing or sales strategies which might affect cash flow?

You should now have enough information to write your letter to the company or to make your presentation.

Extension tasks

- What are the consequences of incorrect forecasts?
- As a potential investor in the Young Enterprise company, what additional information, financial or otherwise, would you want before deciding whether to part with your money?
- If you had access to the final accounts of the company, which ratios could you use to assess its liquidity, profitability and performance? What range of answers would you be looking for and why?
- What other difficulties should be considered when forecasting or managing cash flow in different situations?

To help you, think about the problems of complexity, source and timing of inflows and outflows in the following cases:

– the Walt Disney Company setting up Disneyland Paris,
– a large housebuilder's costs and sales when there is a sudden, sharp rise in interest rates,
– the cyclical nature of, say, fruit picking,
– the local council forecasting in an election year,
– research and development in the pharmaceuticals industry.

Working back to the work force

Your task

In 1997, the retailing chain and financial services provider Marks and Spencer plc had 68 208 employees engaged throughout its UK stores, head office, and financial services and overseas divisions.

The equivalent number of full-time employees was 45 805. This compares to 65 498 employees (being equivalent to 43 773 full-time employees) in 1996. The remuneration and cost of employees was £922.4 million in 1997 and £853.8 million in 1996. The Marks and Spencer Board also provided staff with additional information in the form of the consolidated profit and loss account for the year ended 31 March 1997.

> Write and illustrate a two-page report for employees, who may also be shareholders, explaining how their company has performed over the year to 31 March 1997. (When making comparisons, you should use the information provided for the year to 31 March 1996.)

Datafile

Table 1

Consolidated profit and loss accounts

For year ending	31 March 1997 £m	31 March 1996 £m
Turnover	7841.9	7233.7
Less cost of sales	5103.8	4720.5
Gross profit	2738.1	2513.2
Less expenses (including depreciation: 1997 £162.8m, 1996 £124.8m)	1700.2	1575.8
Operating profit	1037.9	937.4
Loss on disposal of discontinued operations	–	(25)
Loss on sale of property and other fixed assets	(1.8)	(4.2)
Net interest income	65.9	57.6
Profit on ordinary activities before taxation	1102.0	965.8
Taxation	(346.1)	(312.0)
Profit on ordinary activities after taxation	755.9	653.8
Minority interests (all equity)	(1.3)	(1.2)
Profit attributable to shareholders	754.6	652.6
Dividends	(368.6)	(320.9)
Undistributed surplus for the year	386.0	331.7

Table 2

Earnings and productivity

	1997	1996
Earnings per share	26.7p	23.3p
Number of 25p ordinary shares in issue	2 836 658 116	2 815 468 956
Retail productivity		
Group sales per full-time equivalent employee	£166 900	£162 300
Group operating profit per full-time equivalent employee	£21 000	£20 300
Return on retail space		
Group sales per square foot	£562.10	£540.30
Group operating profit per square foot	£70.70	£67.50

Table 3

Group balance sheets as at 31 March 1997

	£m (1997)	£m (1996)
Tangible fixed assets	3609.9	3428.4
Fixed asset investments	36.6	46.0
Current assets	3204.2	2875.5
Total assets	6850.7	6349.9
Creditors due within one year	(1775.1)	(1674.9)
Total assets less current liabilities	5075.6	4675.0
Creditors due after more than one year	(495.8)	(497.8)
Provisions for liabilities and charges	(31.8)	(35.0)
Net assets	4548.0	4142.2

Table 4

Capital and reserves as at 31 March 1997

	£m (1997)	£m (1996)
Called up share capital	709.2	703.9
Share premium account	259.8	221.4
Revaluation reserve	456.3	449.8
Profit and loss account	3104.0	2744.5
Shareholders' funds	4529.3	4119.6
Minority interests	18.7	22.6
Total capital employed	4548.0	4142.2

Table 5

Value added statement of Marks and Spencer plc for year ended 31 March 1996

	£m
Turnover	7233.7
Less losses (£25m + £4.2m)	(29.2)
Add interest income	57.6
	7262.1
Less all other costs	5317.7
= Value added	1944.4

Cost of sales	£4720.5m
Expenses	£1575.8m
= Total costs	£6296.3m

These costs are made up as follows:

Wages, salaries, etc.	£853.8m
Depreciation	£124.8m
All other costs	£5317.7m

Source (Tables 1–5): Marks and Spencer plc, *Annual Report 1997*

Getting started

What is the difference between an employee and a full-time equivalent employee?

What is the average wage per full-time equivalent employee in 1996 and in 1997? What is the percentage change in this figure?

See Units 4 and 14 on averages and percentage changes.

Work out the percentage change in sales per employee and operating profit per employee and compare it to the percentage change in the average wage per employee.

To illustrate the contribution that different factors of production make, firms construct value added statements. An example of a value added statement for Marks and Spencer plc appears in Table 5. The figures are applied as follows:

		£m	£m
To pay employees:	*wages, salaries, etc.*		*853.8*
To pay providers of capital:	*dividends*	*320.9*	
	minority interests	*1.2*	*322.1*
To pay government:	*corporation tax*		*312.0*
To provide for maintenance of assets and expansion of business:			
	depreciation	*124.8*	
	retained earnings	*331.7*	*456.5*
= Value added			*1944.4*

Prepare a value added statement for 1997 and, as some employees may have difficulty interpreting the statement, also provide a pie chart or a stacked bar graph.

When writing your introduction, avoid phrases like 'employees are the most important assets of a firm'. Use the figures you have calculated to emphasise the importance of employees, the returns they have received, the value they have added, and the percentage increases achieved by the firm resulting in wage increases for employees.

Going further

Employees of Marks and Spencer plc can also be shareholders in the company. As a result, they are interested in profitability, liquidity and an assessment of whether their shares are a good investment or not. Make a list of the ratios that assess these aspects of a firm.

When using ratios in examinations, remember to name the ratio, state the model you are using and show all steps in the calculation. Rounding to one decimal place should be sufficient.

Some examples of relevant ratios are calculated below for 1996. Use your list of ratios to calculate the relevant figures for 1997, paying particular attention to the way you set them out.

To assess profitability:

$$\text{gross margin} = \frac{\text{gross profit}}{\text{turnover}} \times \frac{100}{1} = \frac{2513.2}{7233.7} \times \frac{100}{1} = 34.7\%$$

$$\text{net margin} = \frac{\text{operating profit}}{\text{turnover}} \times \frac{100}{1} = \frac{937.4}{7233.7} \times \frac{100}{1} = 13.0\%$$

$$\text{profit margin} = \frac{\text{profit before taxation}}{\text{turnover}} \times \frac{100}{1} = \frac{965.8}{7233.7} \times \frac{100}{1} = 13.4\%$$

$$\text{return on capital employed (ROCE)} = \frac{\text{profit before taxation}}{\text{capital employed}} \times \frac{100}{1}$$

$$= \frac{965.8}{4142.2} \times \frac{100}{1} = 23.4\%$$

There are a number of different models of ROCE. In this case, the firm has no long-term capital, so profit before interest is not very relevant. The interest here is income for the firm. An alternative might be:

$$\text{return on equity} = \frac{\text{profit after tax and minority interests}}{\text{shareholders' funds}} \times \frac{100}{1}$$

$$= \frac{652.6}{4119.6} \times \frac{100}{1} = 15.8\%$$

To assess resource utilisation:

$$\text{utilisation of fixed assets} = \frac{\text{turnover}}{\text{fixed assets}} = \frac{7233.7}{3428.4} = 2.1 \text{ times}$$

$$\text{utilisation of current assets} = \frac{\text{turnover}}{\text{current assets}} = \frac{7233.7}{2875.5} = 2.5 \text{ times}$$

$$\text{utilisation of capital employed} = \frac{\text{turnover}}{\text{capital employed}} = \frac{7233.7}{4142.2} = 1.75 \text{ times.}$$

This means that for every £100 of capital employed, £175 of sales were generated.

To assess liquidity:

current ratio = current assets : current liabilities = 2875.5 : 1674.9 = 1.72 : 1.

To assess investment potential:

$$\text{dividend per share} = \frac{\text{total ordinary share dividend}}{\text{number of ordinary shares in issue}} = \frac{£320.9m}{2815.468\,956 \text{ million}}$$

$$= 11.4p \text{ per share}$$

(be careful with the millions – not all the digits will fit into your calculator)

$$\text{dividend cover} = \frac{\text{profit attributable to shareholders}}{\text{dividends}} = \frac{652.6}{320.9} = 2.0 \text{ times.}$$

Explain to shareholders how to calculate a price/earnings ratio and its relevance. You might also explain a calculation of a dividend yield as this will depend on the price shareholders paid for their shares.

Drawing conclusions

Write a paragraph outlining the performance of Marks and Spencer plc in 1997. Write a further paragraph illustrating the improvement in performance of the company between 1996 and 1997.

A shareholder employee might want answers to the following:
- Why are all the profits not paid out in dividends or as wages?
- Why does the firm have such large retained earnings and how do I benefit from this?
- Why are the earnings per share greater than the dividends per share?

Explain to employees who are not shareholders the benefits of becoming shareholders. In 1997 Marks and Spencer plc allocated £23.5m to a profit-sharing scheme and 11 605 097 shares at an option price of 389p (a 20% discount on the market price) to employees.

You should now have enough information to write your report.

You could use a similar report structure in examinations of introduction, calculation and comment on ratios and evaluation of information, all with a target group in mind.

Evaluating the data

Published accounts may be a narrow basis for judging the performance of a company. What are the limitations of published accounts?

Do the ratios tell you the causes of good or bad performance for a company? Explain your answer.

What other relevant information would you require to make a complete assessment of the performance of Marks and Spencer plc for 1997?

Extension tasks

- Research the accounts of other firms in a similar line of business to Marks and Spencer plc.

This would allow you to produce an inter-firm comparison. Information is available through the Internet. The Marks and Spencer web site is http://www.marks-and-spencer.co.uk if you want to update information as further years' accounts are published. Other company information is available through Biz/ed at http://www.bized.ac.uk/.

- Work out the ratios for firms in different industries.

Be aware of the type of industry you are dealing with. For example, you did not calculate many liquidity ratios in the Marks and Spencer plc report as the firm is getting cash in all the time. Also, the company is structured with ordinary share capital and so gearing was not an issue.

In this section you will:

▶ calculate and comment on price elasticity of demand, income elasticity of demand and cross price elasticity of demand,

▶ comment on how national trends might change the way cinemas compete.

Your task

The British film industry is enjoying a renaissance in film production, with 128 titles produced in 1996 at a cost of £759.2m compared to 60 titles in 1990 at a cost of £262.9m (constant 1997 prices). Despite this, the last remaining cinema in Macclesfield (the Majestic Picture House which opened in 1922) closed in March 1998 to be turned into a pub and nightclub.

> You have been asked to participate in a radio interview on the rebirth of the British film industry. You will be asked to comment on the cinema industry, the economic factors influencing why people go to the cinema in the UK and the way the industry is likely to respond to the growing competitive pressures on it. Make up a concise list of your arguments, supported by analysis of trends in the entertainment industry.

Datafile

Table 1

UK consumer spending on feature films, 1990–96 (all figures £m at current prices)

year	UK box office	video rental	video retail	movie channel subscription	total
1990	273	550	365	47	1235
1991	295	540	444	121	1400
1992	291	511	400	283	1485
1993	319	528	643	350	1840
1994	364	438	698	540	2040
1995	385	789*	457	721**	2352
1996	426	491	803	1319	3039

* Only a portion of the UK video retail market is accounted for by feature films.
** Based on a subscription of £21.99 per month to BSkyB which includes all movie channels but excludes sport.

Source: BFI Film and Television Handbook 1998

Table 2

GB cinema admissions, revenue per admission (nominal and adjusted by GDP deflator), and consumer expenditure in real terms

year	cinema admissions (millions)	revenue per admission (£)	revenue per admission in real terms (constant 1990 prices) (£)	consumer expenditure (constant 1990 prices) (£m)
1990	78.6	2.39	2.39	347527
1991	88.9	2.58	2.44	340037
1992	89.4	2.73	2.46	339652
1993	99.3	2.73	2.38	348015
1994	105.9	2.77	2.37	356914
1995	96.9	2.96	2.50	363810
1996	112.1	3.06	2.48	374811

Sources: Office for National Statistics, Annual Abstract of Statistics 1998;
Economic Review Data Supplement, September 1997

Table 3

Frequency of cinema-going, 1996

Age/group	7–14	15–24	25–34	35+	ABC1	C2DE
No. of people (millions)	5.77	7.19	9.16	29.63	25.42	26.33
Twice a month or more (%)	11	17	7	2	7	4
Once a month (%)	15	22	12	5	11	8
Once every 2–3 months (%)	27	24	22	7	17	11
2–3 times a year (%)	27	20	23	13	18	17
Less often (%)	15	11	24	31	27	24

Source: Adapted from *BFI Film and Television Handbook 1998*

Table 4

UK cinema circuits (s = sites; scr = screens)

year	ABC		Virgin		Cine UK		Odeon		Showcase		UCI		Warner Village		Small chains		Independents	
	s	scr	s	scr	s	scr	s	scr	s	scr	s	scr	s	scr	s	scr	s	scr
1994			119	402			76	327	11	141	26	232	10	93	55	143	437	–
1995			116	406			71	320	11	143	26	232	12	110	57	130	469	–
1996	92	244	24	162	2	24	73	362	14	181	26	232	16	143	58	139	437	–

Table 5

UK cinema advertising revenue, 1990–96

year	£m	year	£m
1990	39	1993	50
1991	42	1994	53
1992	45	1995	69
		1996	73

Table 6

UK video market

year	retail transactions (millions)	value (£m)	rental transactions (millions)	value (£m)
1990	40	374	374	564
1991	45	440	337	554
1992	48	506	317	511
1993	60	643	328	528
1994	66	698	194	438
1995	73	789	194	457
1996	79	803	230	491

Table 7

Cable and satellite penetration, 1996

	cable	satellite
Number of subscribers (millions)	2.24	3.79
Penetration (%)*	10	17

* Represents national figure. There is a 22.4% take-up in cabled areas.

Source (Tables 4–7): BFI Film and Television Handbook 1998

Table 8

In 1994, 96% of UK households had a colour television while 76% had a video recorder.

Source: Office for National Statistics, Social Trends 28, 1998

25% of a cinema's revenue comes from items other than cinema admissions.

Getting started

Describe the trend in admissions to cinemas between 1990 and 1996. Make use of the figures in Table 2 to work out the overall percentage change.

Describe the frequency of cinema-going in 1996 by both age and social class, using Table 3.

Describe the trend in UK box office takings from Table 1 giving both the absolute change and the percentage change in takings between 1990 and 1996.

> *Remember that*
>
> $$percentage\ change = \frac{difference}{original}$$
>
> *The answers to these questions would enable you to respond to an opening interview question on the state of the cinema industry since 1990.*

Going further

How might cinema admissions and price of tickets be related?

> *Think about what you would expect from a demand curve and see if this matches up to the evidence in Table 2. You may have to suggest a hypothesis in terms of real rather than nominal prices. Perhaps the evidence only supports your hypothesis in particular years.*

Can you now put a numerical value on the relationship?

> *Between 1992 and 1993 the real price fell from £2.46 to £2.38 while the number of admissions rose from 89.4m to 99.3m. The price elasticity of demand could be calculated from this information as follows:*
>
> $$\frac{\%\ change\ in\ quantity\ demanded}{\%\ change\ in\ price} = \frac{\dfrac{99.3m - 89.4m}{89.4m} \times \dfrac{100}{1}}{\dfrac{£2.46 - £2.38}{£2.46} \times \dfrac{100}{1}} = \frac{11.07}{3.25} = 3.4$$
>
> *As the answer is greater than 1, it is said that demand does respond to price changes and is elastic.*

Calculate price elasticity of demand for 1993–4, 1994–5 and 1995–6 using real prices and admissions given in Table 2.

Is there a relationship between admissions and consumers' expenditure (which we may have to take as an alternative to income)? Try calculating the income elasticity of demand.

Between 1990 and 1996 cinema admissions went up from 78.6m to 112.1m while consumers' expenditure rose from £347 527m to £374 811m.

$$\frac{\%\ change\ in\ quantity\ demanded}{\%\ change\ in\ consumer's\ expenditure} = \frac{\dfrac{112.1 - 78.6}{78.6} \times \dfrac{100}{1}}{\dfrac{374\,811 - 347\,527}{347\,527}} = \frac{42.62}{7.85} = 5.43$$

Since admissions increase as income increases, cinema admissions are said to be a normal good (if admissions fell as income increased, then they would be said to be an inferior good). In this case, there is a relatively strong relationship between demand for cinema tickets and consumers' expenditure.

Consider whether the same relationship holds between 1990 and 1991, and 1994 and 1995.

What alternative ways do people have of watching feature films besides going to the cinema?

What has happened to the average price of (a) retail purchase of videos and (b) rental of videos?

Using the 1990 row in Table 6: in the retail sector the total value of 40m transactions was £374m so the average price per transaction was

$$\frac{£374m}{40m} = £9.35.$$

Remember that your answers will be in current prices rather than real prices.

Work out the cross price elasticity of demand between cinema admissions and (a) the retail price of videos and (b) the rental price of videos between 1990 and 1996.

Cross price elasticity of demand (with respect to retail price of videos)

$$= \frac{\%\ change\ in\ cinema\ admissions}{\%\ change\ in\ retail\ price\ of\ videos}$$

If the answer is positive, then the goods are said to be substitutes, and if negative, then they are complements.

Why might the cross price elasticity of demand not be a good indicator of changes in the number of people going to the cinema?

If you decide that working out figures here is not very useful, you might describe the influence that videos, television, cable and satellite have on the number of people going to the cinema.

You should now be able to answer specific questions on the economic factors influencing why people go to the cinema. There are also likely to be social factors to take account of as well. Try drafting responses to questions like:
- *What factors influence cinema admissions?*
- *How important are prices and incomes in the decision to go to the cinema?*
- *What impact has the video revolution had on cinema admissions?*
- *What impact do you anticipate the cable and satellite revolution having on cinema admissions?*

Drawing conclusions

Now, you need to think about the impact that the trends you have outlined in the answers to the above questions will have on the way cinemas compete for customers.

Using Table 4, suggest what has happened already in the cinema industry, particularly in terms of the average number of screens per site in the UK.

What advantages do the likes of ABC, Odeon and UCI gain over independents and small chains by building multiplex cinemas on out-of-town and shopping-centre sites?

What changes in society over the past ten years have encouraged the development of out-of-town and shopping-centre sites?

How might the development of multiplex cinemas, offering an 'entertainment experience', shield the cinemas from the effects of price competition and the attractiveness of home entertainment?

Given the calculations you have made, how would you expect cinemas to compete on price? Would it be a good idea to increase or decrease price to raise revenue? Could cinemas subsidise their main product with profits from other areas in order to compete against the home entertainment threat? What implications do your calculations have for cinema managers in terms of location, income group of customers and location of cinemas?

You should now be able to answer questions on the way in which you expect the cinema industry in the UK to develop and compete in the future.

Evaluating the data

To what extent did the data prove a limitation in trying to discover what has caused the change in cinema admissions?

Consider the difficulties you have had in interpreting the data.

Would you now consider that elasticity calculations are more relevant to specific firms' circumstances? Justify your answer.

How much more difficult did you find preparing an oral rather than a written presentation?

Extension tasks

- Explain how you might formulate a marketing mix to help the cinema industry survive competition from other leisure activities. If you have access to the Time 100 series, then the case study on UCI may be another useful source of information.
- The French government taxes foreign-made films to protect its own film industry. Considering the cultural differences between the UK and France, to what extent would a similar policy in the UK work to protect the UK film industry? Carefully consider the effects of this policy on the cinema industry.

Bottle it

In this section you will:

▶ develop ideas on the application of the elasticity concept,

▶ use qualitative information to help design a promotional strategy,

▶ suggest ways of placing your promotion ideas.

Your task

In the UK, a new brand of bottled water appears every ten days. The market for bottled water is about 800 million litres a year, and is growing rapidly, but with a choice of still or sparkling, mineral or spring, natural or flavoured and branded or own-brand, the market is a difficult one in which to place a product. After all, consumers have access to tap water costing 0.07p per litre while the average price for bottled water is 50p per litre.

> As the marketing director of a bottled-water firm, write a report outlining how you are going to capitalise on the lighter-user end of the bottled-water market.

Datafile

Table 1

Bottled-water users are significantly more likely to agree with the following propositions than the rest of the population:

'My diet is mainly vegetarian.'

'I try to take more than one holiday abroad a year.'

'I enjoy films at the cinema more than on TV.'

'I am prepared to pay more for good wine.'

'I enjoy eating foreign food.'

Table 2

Bottled water frequency and volume consumption

	heavy	medium	light	total
% all adults	4.4	9	19	$32\frac{1}{2}$
% of users	14	28	58	100
% volume	46	45	9	100

Source: *Harpers* magazine, 6 January 1995

Table 3

Bottled-water users' age profile

	1984 %	1994 %
15–24	20.5	20.4
25–34	20.2	21.6
35–44	17.0	18.1
45–54	15.5	15.9
55–64	13.5	11.1
65+	13.2	12.9

Source: *Harpers* magazine, 6 January 1995

Table 4

Light bottled-water users

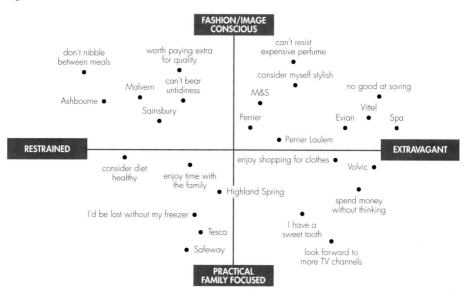

Source: 1994 TGI; BMRB International

Table 5

UK bottled-water market, 1980–2000

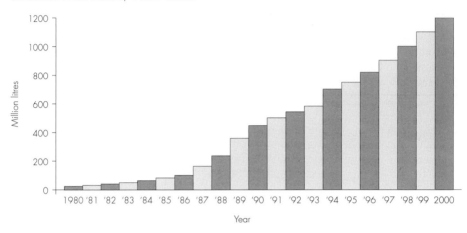

Source: 1994 TGI; BMRB International

Table 6

Demographics: bottled-water users – social grade profile, Great Britain

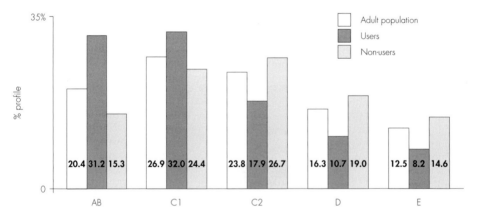

Source: 1994 TGI; BMRB International

Table 7

Market changes by type: % volume, all trade sectors

	1989	1993	1994
Still	43	60	62
Sparkling	57	40	38
Natural mineral	94	73	68
Spring/others	6	27	32
Brand	82	80	79
Own-brand	18	20	21
Natural	96	97	97
Flavoured	4	3	3

Source: *Harpers* magazine, 6 January 1995

The price of sparking water has fallen 15% year on year.

In 1994 total sales volume grew by 17% (helped by a good summer) and retail prices fell because of the introduction of cheap spring water, more frequent price promotion and greater sales of value multi-packs.

Getting started

Estimate the market value of the bottled-water market. Assuming prices remain the same, use Table 5 to estimate the value of the market by 2000.

What percentage of the adult population consumes bottled water (see Table 2)?

Describe the changes that have taken place in the bottled-water market between 1989 and 1994 using Table 7. What is the typical age for bottled-water drinkers?

The answers to these questions, and task, are likely to provide you with a short introduction to your report. Re-read the information given here and see if there is anything else that you might add to your introduction.

Going further

> *The data given here require you to think carefully about the people who are currently light users of bottled water. You also need to think through ideas which might be useful in gaining a market share. (The relevant piece of theory might be 'the four Ps'.)*

Write a sentence summarising the information in Table 2 with reference to light bottled-water users.

Demographic information suggests that bottled-water users are upmarket. What does this suggest about income sensitivity? Use the other information given, particularly in Table 7, to suggest what price sensitivity might be.

> *Here you are talking about the responsiveness of demand to two major influences – price and income. You are saying something about elasticity.*
>
> *Look at the information on brand/own-brand. Remember that 1989 to 1993 is a four-year gap so the average percentage increase/decrease is the difference between the figures divided by four.*
>
> *Perhaps some of the information in Table 1 would allow you to make assumptions about what products would go with and/or provide an alternative to bottled water.*

Summarise your ideas on the price sensitivity of light users. Using Tables 1 and 4, list in order of importance the factors that are likely to influence the promotion of bottled water to users.

> *In Table 4 the closer someone is to the cross-over between the lines, the closer they are to being the typical light user.*

Which product variation are you going to aim for? Justify your answer.

> *You should now have outlined the major areas of your report.*

Drawing conclusions

Would you suggest promoting a branded product or seeking a tie-up with an own-brand label?

Consider your ideas on price, income, other related products and market trends.

Revisit your list of promotional factors. Justify the top three points on your list and use them to outline how these points can be used to capture your target audience. How might you go about promoting your product? Consider the ways suggested by the data, e.g. cinema rather than TV advertising. Suggest some advertising slogans that would reflect the concerns of consumers. Consider the distribution chain for your product – you do not have to use the usual grocery retail outlets.

How do you direct the promotion at potential customers? How can the age profile be tied up with the life style statements? Could you segment the market into sections and use a different promotional strategy in each? How might you use packaging of the product to capture some of the important characteristics of the market?

What conclusions can you draw from the information which must be considered in marketing your product?

Try to conclude in no more than 200–250 words as this will help you concentrate on the main points.

Evaluating the data

While some of this information may be considered historic, to what extent do the data suggest stability in the bottled-water market and so continue to be of use?

How might you use the ideas you have developed in this unit to begin thinking about other products such as carbonated soft drinks, cordials and other still soft drinks? To what extent are these products similar/different? If you were a marketing manager commissioning market research into these areas, what types of information would you want to have?

Is there any further information you would require for a complete picture of the bottled-water market?

Extension tasks

- Consider how competitors would react to your launching a new product.
- Consider the impact on the profitability of your firm should the price of packaging increase. Use your ideas on price elasticity and its relationship with total revenue.
- Design and suggest a placing for a print advertisement for your product. If you have access to a personal computer, then produce one.

Beyond your control?

In this section you will:

► use data to analyse the effect of economic variables on business,

► develop an understanding of the interrelationship between these variables and business and its performance,

► use these trends to predict future outcomes.

Your task

You have been employed as an economist for the UK government. One of your first tasks is to analyse the state of the UK economy over the period 1980–96.

Produce an analytical report which addresses the following issues:
- the level of consumer confidence in the economy,
- the relationship between economic growth and inflation,
- the effects of economic growth on the balance of payments.

Datafile

Table 1

Real incomes and consumer spending, 1992–96 (£bn at 1990 prices)

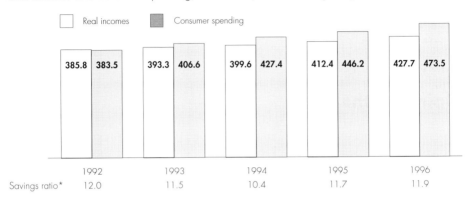

| Real incomes | Consumer spending |

	1992	1993	1994	1995	1996
Real incomes	385.8	393.3	399.6	412.4	427.7
Consumer spending	383.5	406.6	427.4	446.2	473.5
Savings ratio*	12.0	11.5	10.4	11.7	11.9

*as a percentage of real income
Source: Office for National Statistics, *Annual Abstract of Statistics 1998*

Table 2

year	UK economic growth, 1980–96	UK inflation, 1980–96	UK current balance of payments, 1980–96
	% per annum	annual % change	% of GDP
1980	−1.6	16.3	1.5
1981	−1.3	11.2	2.5
1982	1.6	8.7	1.5
1983	3.5	4.8	0.8
1984	2.5	5.0	−0.3
1985	3.5	5.3	0.3
1986	4.4	4.0	−1.1
1987	4.8	4.3	−2.2
1988	5.0	5.0	−4.9
1989	2.2	5.9	−5.6
1990	0.4	5.5	−4.9
1991	−2.0	7.4	−2.7
1992	−0.5	4.7	−2.6
1993	2.1	3.5	−2.5
1994	3.9	2.5	−2.1
1995	2.5	2.6	−2.3
1996	2.4	2.7	−2.3

Source: SECOS datasets

Getting started

Study Tables 1 and 2 and examine what underlying trends exist in either the data or the diagram. Think carefully about the relationships between these variables – how do they affect one another?

Consult the glossary in your textbook if you are having difficulties with any of the terms used in the tables.

Going further

Describe the trends experienced in the UK from 1992 to 1996, i.e. real incomes and consumer expenditure (see Table 1). Suggest reasons for the growth of consumer expenditure exceeding the growth of real incomes. Describe the state of the economy over this time period. What would be the effect on businesses in the UK/the rest of the world?

Examine the rate of economic growth, shown in Table 2, over the period 1980–96. Plot the data on to a line graph. Can you see the shape of the business cycle emerging? Highlight the peak and boom years.

Plot the rate of inflation, shown in Table 2, over the period 1980–96 on to a line graph. How has the rate of inflation changed over the time period? What factors may have caused the level of inflation to rise and fall?

Examine the figures shown in Table 2 for the UK's balance of payments over this time period. When was the UK running a balance of payments deficit? Describe the relationship between the strength of the UK pound and the level of exports and imports bought and sold over this time period.

Drawing conclusions

You should now be able to begin to draw together all the data.

Remember that consumer spending and real income are not the only components that make up economic growth.

Begin by comparing Table 1 with the economic growth figures in Table 2. Do they both follow the same pattern? If not, why not? What other factors may be an influence here?

Evaluating the data

Compare the first two columns in Table 2. Describe the relationship between economic growth and inflation – you may wish to plot both variables on the same graph. What pattern is emerging?

Compare the first and last columns in Table 2. What tends to happen to the balance of payments situation when the UK experiences a positive rate of economic growth? Why is this the case?

Estimate the trend of interest rates over the period 1980–96. Explain why interest rates behave in the way you suggest. What is the relationship between interest rates, economic growth and inflation? How does the level of interest rates affect the behaviour of British business?

Extension tasks

- Compare the UK economy with other economies in this time period. Are the trends similar throughout other countries? Why might this be the case?
- Name an economy with an unstable rate of economic growth. What might the effect of this be on consumer confidence?
- Estimate the level of UK economic growth up to and including 2002. What pattern do you expect it to take? Explain your reasons.

Ringing the changes

Your task

Mohan has just bought Sigma Dry Cleaners, an established dry-cleaning business. While Mohan has previous retail and computing experience, he has no direct experience of the dry-cleaning market. He also realises that the cash till he has inherited needs replacing and is considering two options for its replacement.

As Mohan's adviser, write a report to him recommending one of the tills on the basis of accounting rate of return (ARR), payback period and net present value (NPV). Advise Mohan on the viability of the loyalty card scheme. Besides financial calculations you should include other relevant factors in reaching a decision.

Datafile

Table 1

Comparison of till types 1 and 2

	till type 1	till type 2
Cost	£3550	£1540
Useful economic life	3 years	3 years
Depreciation	$33\frac{1}{3}$% per year on cost	20% per year on cost
Till functions	Records cash taken	Records cash taken
	Produces printed cleaning tickets and customer copy	Produces printed cleaning tickets and customer copy
	Produces graphs of sales	Monitors staff control of the till
	Produces management accounts such as profit and loss	
	Holds details of customers	
Training	Manual provided	Manual provided
Time saving on administration*	$1\frac{1}{2}$ hours per day	$\frac{1}{2}$ hour per day
Scrap value at end of 3 years	Nil	£600

*Assume that administration time saved can be used to process dry-cleaning items

Table 2

Till type 1 will accept a loyalty card, which Mohan is considering. Each card costs 58p and Mohan is thinking of initially getting 100 cards. He hopes to generate an extra 70 customers per week, each spending £2.80. For this, he is thinking of giving each customer a discount of 2p for every £1 spent.

Table 3

Mohan works six days a week and pays his staff £6 per hour. His business is currently earning a rate of return of 10%.

Mohan will use the time saved on administration to work in the dry-cleaning area to replace existing staff hours.

Table 4

Discount rate at 10%:

Year 1   0.909
Year 2   0.826
Year 3   0.751

Getting started

Outline the accounting rate of return, the payback period and the net present value methods of capital appraisal, clearly explaining the difference between cash flow and profits.

> *Consult the glossary in your textbook if you are having difficulties with any of these terms. It is useful to learn definitions with examples to illustrate them.*

What advantages does till type 1 have over till type 2 (see Table 1)? Are there any potential disadvantages of till type 1?

Going further

> *You might find it useful to consider each appraisal method in turn for each till. The time saving per day for each till needs to be valued first.*

What value will you put on the time? What then is the saving per year (given that there are 52 weeks in a year)?

The accounting rate of return requires a calculation of the depreciation each year for each till. Use the percentages given in Table 1 to calculate these figures.

The till itself is an administrative item, as it does not actually sell dry cleaning. Consequently, the profit on the till should be the time saving less the depreciation charge. Work this out for each year.

> *This calculation gives the average profit.*

What is the capital employed for tills 1 and 2? Remember that with till 2 there is a scrap value at the end of the three years.

Now work out the ARR using the formula:

$$\frac{\text{average profit}}{\text{capital employed}} \times \frac{100}{1}$$

Calculate the payback period for each till only from the savings made.

Why is depreciation not taken into account here? Remember that the £600 for till 2 only comes in at the end of year 3 so it is not relevant to the calculations.

For the payback method, add the savings until you come up to the capital cost. This will happen between years 1 and 2.

Use the discount rate given in Table 4 to calculate the net present value of each project based on the yearly saving.

You might like to set this out as follows:

year	till 1 cash flow	till 2 cash flow	discount factor	net cash flows till 1	till 2
0 (present)	Negative cost outflow	Negative cost outflow	1	Discount factor multiplied by the relevant saving cash flow	
1	Positive saving	Saving inflow	0.909		
2	inflow each		0.826		
3	year	Last year: remember the positive inflow from the scrap value	0.751		

You could also set up a spreadsheet to do the calculations for you. This would be useful if you changed the discount factor, say in trying to find the internal rate of return.

Drawing conclusions

You should now have enough information to write your report to Mohan.

On the basis of each method of appraisal, recommend which till Mohan should purchase. Explain what an accounting rate of return higher than the business is presently achieving will do to its profitability.

Explain in the report why cash flows rather than profits are a more appropriate way of appraising an investment.

Suggest reasons why the net present value method might be the best method on which to make a decision.

Explain any reservations you may have about the data you have been provided with.

Advise Mohan as to any other factors you consider relevant in reaching a decision.

If Mohan were to purchase till type 1, how might you reappraise the investment decision on the basis of including the information on the loyalty card option (Table 2)?

> Here is some further information to help you:
>
> Mohan's net cash inflow is about 45p per £2.80 dry-cleaning item. This is before his proposed discount. Assume that the cost of the till and cards is paid out now and that the other costs and revenues all occur on the last day of the accounting year. Remember that the cash inflow has to be adjusted for the discount he proposes to give.

Do you recommend that Mohan should go ahead with the loyalty card option on the basis of the net present value method? What other advantages would a loyalty card scheme offer the business?

Evaluating the data

To what extent would an investment decision like this be analysed in this way by a small business? What are the potential disadvantages for a small business of not using a capital investment appraisal method?

To what extent is it realistic to suggest that the administration time saved would be used in processing dry-cleaning items?

Extension tasks

- Set up a spreadsheet to find the internal rate of return on the loyalty card option.
- Evaluate the extent to which technological change may be a hindrance rather than a help to the small business.
- Try another net present value evaluation on the following information. A firm is considering the purchase of a new plant in either the UK or Germany:

(a) The capital cost of the UK plant is £4m and the German plant £3.35m.

(b) The UK government is prepared to offer a subsidy of £0.5m to the firm if it locates in the UK.

(c) The cash flows from both plants are as follows:

year	UK plant inflow	outflow	German plant inflow	outflow
1	£980 000	£250 000	£820 000	£490 000
2	£1 970 000	£450 000	£1 350 000	£620 000
3	£2 340 000	£720 000	£1 820 000	£900 000
4	£2 340 000	£780 000	£1 950 000	£910 000
5	£1 620 000	£700 000	£1 100 000	£400 000

It should be assumed that the cash inflows and outflows occur at the end of the relevant year.

(d) The firm expects that in year 3 the pound will fall in value, thus increasing the net cash flows from the German plant by the following amounts:

Year 3   £310 000
Year 4   £400 000
Year 5   £320 000

(e) The company cost of capital is 10%, and the relevant extract from the discount tables is:

	10% discount factor
Year 1	0.909
Year 2	0.826
Year 3	0.751
Year 4	0.683
Year 5	0.621

• Use the above figures to evaluate the project using the payback method.

Decision time

In this section you will:

▶ identify the types of problems suitable for decision trees,

▶ be aware of the rules of drawing decision trees,

▶ understand how the idea of probability is used in making the decision,

▶ perform the calculations required for this technique.

Your task (1)

Without wishing to lead you into bad practices, let us imagine you are standing in a queue for the bookmakers on the day before the Grand National. In one race, there are three horses, each with different odds.

> On which one would you place a £10 bet?

Datafile

Table 1

Speedy (a pedigree racehorse with a superb record): 5–1
Unreliable (soon to go into retirement after a glittering career): 10–1
Always Last (a donkey ridden by a 15-stone man): 100–1

Getting started

What would happen if the bet was on Speedy? What is the horse's chance of winning? If the same race ran regularly, how would your winnings compare with your lost bets?

Assuming the odds were accurate, this horse has a 20% chance of winning (1 in 5). This means that if the race was run 100 times with the same horse and the same odds and the same bet, it would win on 20 occasions (i.e. 20% of the time). A bet of £10 would attract winnings of £10 × 5 = £50 per race, so 20 wins would lead to:

20 × £50 = £1000.

However, it would lose on 80 occasions, leading to a total loss of:

80 × £10 (the bet) = £800.

Total winnings – total losses = £1000 – £800 = £200.
Over 100 races, this is an average of £2 per race.

This is the net gain of betting on this horse and is known as the **expected value.** *It represents the average amount you would win if the bet was placed 'many' times on the same horse. Of course, the race will only be run once within these parameters, but this is the start of the process.*

Try the same calculation putting £10 on Unreliable and £10 on Always Last. What are the expected values for each horse?

Over 100 races, Unreliable would win 10 times (based on odds of 10–1). Each time you would win £10 × 10 = £100, so the total winning sum would be £100 × 10 = £1000. On the other hand you would lose on 90 occasions so the net gain = £1000–£900 = £100. Over 100 races, the expected gain would be £1.00 per race.

Placing a £10 bet on Always Last would end up with a net gain of £10, which over 100 races represents an expected return of £0.10.

Going further

A shorter method of working out the expected return is to take the actual pay-off (the amount you would end up winning or losing) adjusted by the probability of winning or losing:

horse	probability of winning	total pay-off	probability × winnings
Speedy	0.2	£50	£10
Unreliable	0.1	£100	£10
Always Last	0.01	£1000	£10

The fact these are all £10 is because the size of the bet is the same.

Apply the same calculation to the probability of losing:

horse	probability of losing	actual loss	probability × loss
Speedy	0.8	£10	£8.00
Unreliable	0.9	£10	£9.00
Always Last	0.99	£10	£9.90

For each horse, take the loss from the winnings:

Speedy	*£10–£8*	*=*	*£2*
Unreliable	*£10–£9*	*=*	*£1*
Always Last	*£10–£9.90*	*=*	*£0.10*

*These are the **expected values** of each horse.*

The decision-making process can be modelled in many different ways. One diagrammatic model, developed at the Harvard Business School in the mid 1950s, represents the process as 'decision trees'.

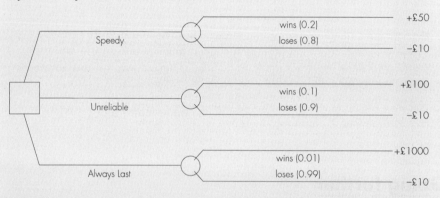

*A **square** indicates that a **decision** is to be made (which horse to choose).*

*A **circle** (or node) represents the risk or uncertainty and the likelihood of something happening. This is shown by the **probability** of occurrence of a decision and therefore requires a calculation.*

Node 1 (Speedy): (£50 × 0.2) + (−£10 × 0.8) = £2
Node 2 (Unreliable): (£100 × 0.1) + (−£10 × 0.9) = £1
Node 3 (Always Last): (£1000 × 0.01) + (−£10 × 0.99) = £0.10

The decision is the one which gives us the largest net gain, i.e. a bet on Speedy.

Such a decision is taken not on the actual gain or loss, but on the gain or loss adjusted by the risk or probability of this happening.

Evaluating the data

How reliable is the estimated value? Is it reasonable to assume that Speedy will perform to the same standard over 100 races?

Decision trees put a value on a decision based on a numerical probability. This modelling has to simplify the real process and in so doing, ignores all the variables which might lead to a different outcome. Horse races vary considerably with weather conditions, with the long-term fitness of the horse and the performance of riders among other things. However, it does allow some kind of careful comparison of options when the alternative would be to work from perhaps inspired guesswork.

*Remember, the decision is made on **average gain**, not on the actual figures.*

Your task (2)

The Board of Directors of Cool Ideas is deciding whether to launch a new product and whether to do so after completing some market research. The market research, costing £12 000, would increase the chance of a successful launch to 70%. Without market research the chance of a successful launch would be 50%. A successful launch would earn £60 000 for the business, but if it failed, only £20 000 would be earned.

As financial director, write a report to the Board recommending the decision it should take. Include in the report how you would go about the decision.

Getting started

Calculate the probability of success and failure in each case. Then draw a decision tree. Work through the information you have been given and make sure your diagram clearly displays the logic of the data. Here is an example of the calculating process:

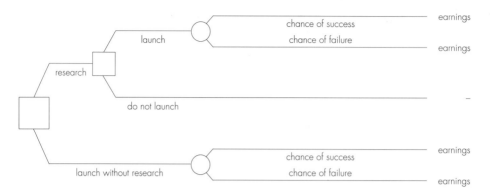

Calculate the expected value of the launch for Nodes 1 and 2:

> *e.g. Node 1: (earnings from success × chance of success) + (earnings from failure × chance of failure) = expected value of the launch*
>
> *The decision at square 1 is whether to launch or not. We must consider the expected value of the launch, to see if it is better than not launching. However, to take the decision at square 2, we must subtract the cost of pre-launch research from the (expected) value of the launch. This figure is then compared with the expected value of launching without the research, to see which is greater.*
>
> *Should the final decision be to launch with or without research?*

Evaluating the data

What assumptions have been made in using this decision-tree model?

> *We are assuming, of course that the forecasted values are correct, and that the probabilities are also correct. Indeed, a change in these probabilities could actually alter the decision! The probabilities can only allow for set outcomes, i.e. either success or failure.*
>
> *The process does not take into account any qualitative information yet there will always be a wide range of non-numerical issues informing business decisions.*

Extension tasks

- Which A-levels? Choosing three from a range of many A-levels could have been a recent decision for you. Try to work out the probability of your best grade and worst grade in each of your subjects, attaching the usual UCAS points per grade – 10 for A, 8 for B, 6 for C, etc. Work out the expected value for each of your subjects. Is the total enough to get you into the university of your first choice?

- A business is deciding how it can achieve growth.

  It could invest in new machinery, although this will need a growing economy (probability = 70%). No growth in the economy means no business investment and no future profits.

  With new investment, profit has a 50% chance of increasing by £30m, a 30% chance of increasing by £10m and a 20% chance of staying the same. The cost of financing the investment will be £10m. Developing the domestic market is more straightforward, with an advertising campaign costing £40m. The chance of success and subsequent profits are as follows:

Success of advertising	high	medium	low
Probability	0.4	0.3	0.3
Profit	£60m	£45m	£20m

Start by giving the decision tree below a quick glance, then try to draw it yourself. Check you have the correct shape, then fill in the actual values and probabilities. What should the final answer be?

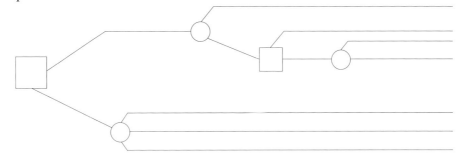

Choosing the right path

In this section you will:

- recognise the types of problems which lend themselves to critical path analysis,
- be able to organise and present data in a diagrammatic form (simple networks),
- perform calculations which help to prioritise decisions,
- understand the significance of critical path analysis in decision-making.

Your task (1)

Detailed planning is required when a business makes a decision involving many activities, e.g. the launch of a new product or the extension of a factory. Critical path analysis (CPA) is a tool which helps the business to focus on the most important activities as well as allowing it to save costs and allocate resources efficiently.

Draw a flow diagram to represent the activities necessary to making a cup of tea. Think about the time it would take to complete the process, including washing cups, filling kettles, etc. Think about how tasks could be ordered to save time.

Datafile

Table 1

Activity	Time taken
A = fill kettle with water	5 seconds
B = clean the cup	5 seconds
C = boil the water	120 seconds
D = find milk	15 seconds
E = find tea bag and put in cup	10 seconds
F = pour boiling water into cup	5 seconds
G = add milk and stir	10 seconds

Getting started

The process of making a cup of tea involves boiling water, putting a tea bag and some milk in a clean cup, pouring the water into the cup and stirring the mixture. Order the activities into a logical sequence. Decide which activities can be carried out at the same time as others and which activities must immediately precede (go before). Assume only one person is making the tea.

Activity	Duration	Preceded by
A = fill kettle with water	5 seconds	–
B = clean the cup	5 seconds	A
C = boil the water	120 seconds	B
D = find milk	15 seconds	B
E = find tea bag and put in cup	10 seconds	D
F = pour boiling water into cup	5 seconds	C,E
G = add milk and stir	10 seconds	F

You will notice in the above table that activities have the duration labelled. Now we need to look more closely at the start times and finish times of each activity. It should be possible to identify the critical time when one process has to be completed before another can begin. This can be represented in a network diagram using some given rules so that the information is clear.

Some basic rules for drawing the network diagrams:

○   a node denotes the start and finish of the network

——————▶ denotes an activity which has a duration

As an example, here is a project with four activities:

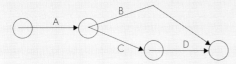

The above means A begins on its own, then B and C may begin once A has finished. D may start once C has finished.

Here is another example where A and B begin together, C follows B, D follows A and E follows C. This project can be represented in diagram form as follows:

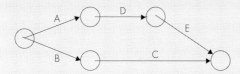

By dividing each node, start and finish times can be incorporated into the network diagram.

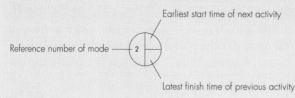

The next network diagram has the numbers for earliest start time and latest finish time filled in. Look carefully at the information and decide
(a) the earliest start time for activity F,
(b) what the latest finish time will be at Node 2.

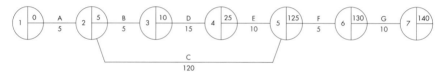

Explanation:
EST of Node 1 = 0 (zero)
EST of Node 2 = 5 (once A has finished)
EST of Node 3 = 10 (once B has finished)
EST of Node 4 = 25 (once D has finished)

Node 5 is the most important. Remember that we are looking at the EST of F which cannot start until both E and C have finished: although E will have finished by 35 seconds, C will not finish until 125 seconds, so the earliest time F can begin is 125 (i.e. the larger of 35 and 125). G can therefore begin at 130 seconds and the last node is 140 seconds, which represents the earliest time the project can finish.

Now look carefully at the Latest Finish Times (LFT); the information you now have is the duration and the earliest start time, but we can also conclude that the LFT of G must be 140 seconds if the project is to finish by that time.

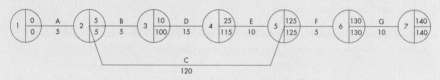

Now we work backwards. If the project is to finish by 140 seconds, F must have a LFT of 140−10 = 130, so E and C must finish by 125. Working backwards, node 4 (LFT of D)

will be 125–10 = 115, and Node 3 must have LFT of 115–15 = 100. This leaves us with Node 2; we must compare the figures from Node 5 because we are looking at activity C. The LFT of B is 125, so Node 2 must have 5 as the LFT. (If we look at Node 3 and Node 2, 100–5 = 95, but if we insert 95 into the LFT of node 2, this will mean C will not finish until 95 + 125, meaning we will not finish within 140 seconds!)

Remember, the language may sound difficult but all the diagram is doing is to apply logical thinking to save time and to prevent unnecessary hold-ups.

Going further

Identify any activities in the tea-making process which will lengthen the project beyond 140 seconds if delayed.

To do this we calculate any 'spare' time which may exist in the process. This is called 'total float' and is the difference between the Latest and the Earliest Start Times. We do not have the LST, so we must use the equivalent which is LFT – duration. Substituting this into the formula gives total float = LFT – duration – EST.

Now we can work this float out for each activity.

	LFT at end of activity	–	duration	–	EST at beginning	=	total float
A	5		5		0		0
B	95		5		5		85
C	125		120		5		0
D	115		15		10		90
E	125		10		25		90
F	130		5		125		0
G	140		10		130		0

*Remember that total float is the 'spare' time available for each activity. Any delay beyond this time will delay the entire project. We see that A, C, F and G have total float of zero meaning that **any delay in these activities will lengthen the process of making a cup of tea beyond 140 seconds**. Hence these activities are known as critical activities and **the critical path is A, C, F, G**. A delay of 5 seconds in activity F would delay the entire project by 5 seconds. However, delaying activity D by 5 seconds would not have any effect on the entire project. Follow this through on the network and you will* *see that the EST of F (Node 5) would still be 125. (It is also shown by D having total float of 90 seconds, so we could delay D by 90 seconds in total and still finish in 140 seconds.)*

Your task (2)

A building company is given a contract to extend a company's factory. Before it presents the quotation for a price it must first work out its costs. Such an extension is likely to engage many different tasks, some of which can occur simultaneously, some of which must take place before others. Each activity will take a certain amount of time, normally in days, and will require labour and materials. Some of the labour will be of a specific skill and will only be required on certain days; having the labour waiting from the start of the building project is clearly a waste of time and costs if that particular skill, e.g. the person who puts felt on the roof, is needed on day 35 of the project. Similarly, the materials for the roof will not be required until that day, so having them delivered on day 1 is money tied up in unproductive assets – something the business will certainly wish to avoid. Critical path analysis will therefore help the business to build the extension in a way which allows it to control costs and resources.

> Draw up a network diagram and establish:
> - the earliest time at which machinery could be installed in the extension;
> - the latest time at which staff hiring and training can begin.

The following activities would be appropriate for such a project:

activity		time taken	preceded by
A	Obtaining planning permission	42 days	–
B	Arranging for land to be levelled and foundations laid	5 days	A
C	Foundations built	5 days	B
D	External walls and roof constructed	21 days	C
E	Road connection between extension and old plant built	10 days	A
F	Air-conditioning and wiring built in	6 days	D
G	Machinery installed for extension	3 days	E, F
H	Extra stocks ordered and delivered for machinery	4 days	G
J	Labour hired and trained	14 days	A
K	Plant performs first production run	1 day	J, H

Taking each activity in turn, sketch out the network in rough first. Draw large nodes to help you and make sure the arrowheads point in the right direction.

Extension tasks

- As an extension activity, show that the minimum duration of this building project is 87 days and that the critical path is A, B, C, D, F, G, H, K.
- Think of another business project that might be appropriate for using critical path analysis. Make a list of the activities and how long each will last. Establish the logical order of each activity, then draw the network diagram to calculate the minimum duration and critical path.

Tucker's Sandwich Bar

In this section you will:

- understand the idea of break even to see how it affects business decisions,
- draw a graph to show the break-even level of output,
- use a formula to calculate the break-even level of output,
- use the idea of margin of safety,
- consider the benefits and limitations of break-even analysis,
- understand the effects of changing variables on the break-even level of output.

Your task

In October 1998 Robert Tucker left a promising career in hotel management to fulfil a lifetime ambition – to own and run his own business. Having often heard his friends in the local building trade bemoaning the lack of cheap sandwich bars catering for workers' breakfasts, Robert saw a gap in the market and opened his own sandwich bar in the centre of town.

At first, business was slow, but soon Robert's sandwich bar was full of customers all asking for the famous Tucker's Topper, an enormous sandwich filled with a fried English breakfast. Robert now faced one problem: had he priced his famous Tucker's Topper correctly so as to cover all of his costs?

> As Robert's accountant, calculate his break-even level of output.

Datafile

Table 1

Ingredients of a Tucker's Topper

1 flatcake (large bread bun)	15p
2 sausages	5p each
4 rashers of bacon	6p each
2 fried eggs	3p each
1 spoonful of beans	3p
2 fried tomatoes	4p each
butter	1p
ketchup/brown sauce	1p
paper bag	2p

Robert has set the price of a Tucker's Topper at £2.50.

Table 2

Tucker's Sandwich Bar: other costs

Rent	£10 000 per year
Council tax	£1100 per year
Electricity	£150 per quarter
Gas	£100 per quarter
Salary	£8000 per year

Getting started

Using Tables 1 and 2, copy and complete the following table with output ranges 0 to 8000 (increasing in 1000s) (round figures to the nearest whole number).

output	variable costs	fixed costs	total costs	total revenue	profit/loss
1000					
⋮					
8000					

In order to complete the table (estimation method), you must calculate the individual variable cost of a Tucker's Topper. Pay close attention to the amount of ingredients required to produce just one of them! Remember that total variable costs increase with the level of output. When completing the fixed costs column, it is important to note the time scales of the different costs and to calculate total fixed costs for one year. The total costs column shows the calculation of the total costs of the Tucker's Topper over varying output levels.

The total revenue column requires you to calculate the total revenue at each output level, bearing in mind that each Tucker's Topper is priced at £2.50.

The profit/loss column requires you to calculate the profit/loss at each output level. It is at this point that you should be examining the figures to see if break-even level of output has been selected, i.e. whether a value of zero has been achieved.

Use these formulae to calculate:

total variable cost = variable cost per unit × output

total fixed costs = sum of individual fixed costs

total costs = total fixed costs + total variable costs

total revenue = price per unit × output

profit/loss = total revenue − total costs.

Does Robert break even over this range of output? How can you tell?

There are three methods you can use to calculate the level of break even. This question deals with the estimation method, i.e. the calculation of profit/loss using varying levels of output in the hope that one of the output levels will be the break-even level – a very risky and time consuming method! The only advantage this method has is that it helps you to understand the calculation of profit/loss and to recognise that the break-even level of output will show a figure of zero in the profit/loss column.

Using the break-even formula and the data in Tables 1 and 2, calculate how many Tucker's Toppers Robert would have to sell in one year to break even.

This question asks you to use the formula method for calculating break even. For this, you must have an understanding of 'contribution'. This is the quickest and simplest of the three methods.

The formula for the calculation of break even is:

total fixed costs/ ÷ contribution
where contribution = price – variable cost per unit.

For example, a business with total fixed costs of £10 000, and a product with variable costs per unit of £5 which sells at a price of £10, will break even at the following level of output:

£10 000 ÷ (£10 – £5) = 2000

Plot fixed costs, total costs and total revenue on a graph, using Tables 1 and 2. Show the break-even level of output.

This question asks you to use the graphical method to identify the level of break even – again a limitation being the accuracy of the graph in showing the exact level.

Going further

The break-even point represents 'the level of output where total cost and total revenue are the same'. Businesses need to be aware of exactly how many of their products/services they need to sell in order to cover all of their costs (both fixed and variable). Firms use break-even analysis in several ways – primarily, to judge profitability and how varying output levels affect the break-even point, but also as a tool for analysing prices and costs. The most common methods of calculating the level of break even involves either a graphical method, which plots total revenue and total costs on the same axes and examines the point of intersection, or working out the level of contribution per product and then dividing this figure into total fixed costs. ('Contribution' is the amount of money left over when the variable cost per unit is subtracted from the selling price.)

For the graphical method, the choice of scale is vital – use your answer from the formula method of calculating break even to decide your range of output.

Plot output on the horizontal axis and costs/revenues on the vertical axis.

Where the total costs curve and total revenue curve intersect will determine the break-even level of output. For example, the graph on page 58 shows the break-even level of output for a firm with fixed costs of £10 000, variable cost per unit of £5 and a selling price of £10 per unit.

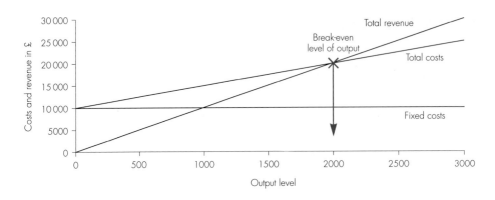

Drawing conclusions

Given that the shop closes every Sunday throughout the year and on Christmas Day, how many Tucker's Toppers would Robert have to sell per day in order to break even?

Is this a realistic amount for Robert to sell in a day?

> There are 365 days in the year and 52 Sundays.

Evaluating the data

> For each of the three methods of calculating break even outlined above, you need to recognise the differing units involved in the ingredients list and in the description of fixed costs.
>
> The task asks for a calculation on a yearly basis and so figures must be calculated on that basis.

Extension tasks

- If Robert manages to sell a total of 15 000 Tucker's Toppers every year, calculate his margin of safety.

> *The margin of safety represents the quantity sold over and above the break-even level where the business makes a profit. It is often shown as a percentage:*
>
> $$\text{margin of safety} = \frac{(\text{actual quantity sold} - \text{break-even quantity})}{\text{break-even quantity}} \times 100\%.$$

- If Robert increased the price of one Tucker's Topper to £3.00, calculate the effect on the break-even level of output.
- If Robert's total fixed costs increase by 10%, explain the effect on the break-even quantity.
- Draw a graph to show the effect of a 10% reduction in total variable costs.
- Is £2.50 a suitable price to charge for a Tucker's Topper? What other factors should Robert take into account when setting the price?
- Discuss the benefits and limitations of break-even analysis in making business decisions.

Getting over a scare

In this section you will:
- use the arithmetic mean,
- calculate a three point moving average,
- offer advice on how to react to changing public opinion.

Your task

The measles/mumps/rubella (MMR) vaccine was introduced in 1988. In 1998 there were newspaper reports linking the MMR vaccine with autism, though the risk was very small. There is also public concern with food-related stories following well-publicised outbreaks of food poisoning.

> As a public relations consultant, write a report to the health service advising it as to the best way to plan and respond to a lack of public confidence in the MMR vaccine and to public concern over food safety.

Datafile

Table 1

Notifications of infectious diseases in the UK, 1989–96

	1989	1990	1991	1992	1993	1994	1995	1996
Measles	31 045	15 642	11 702	12 317	12 017	23 516	9 015	6 865
Mumps	24 505	5 297	3 834	3 169	2 726	3 143	2 397	2 182
Rubella	31 879	15 736	9 702	9 150	12 300	9 650	7 674	11 720
Whooping cough	13 550	16 862	6 270	2 750	4 718	4 837	2 399	2 721
Food poisoning	56 255	55 988	56 136	67 579	72 790	86 890	88 341	89 741
Tuberculosis	6 059	5 897	6 078	6 441	6 564	6 228	6 174	6 238

Source: Office for National Statistics, *Annual Abstract of Statistics*, 1998

Table 2

Immunisation of children in the UK, selected years

	1981	1991–2	1995–6
Whooping cough	45%	88%	94%
Measles, mumps, rubella (includes measles-only vaccine as MMR was not available prior to 1988)	52%	90%	92%

Source: Office for National Statistics, *Social Trends 28*, 1998

Table 3

'Immunisation against whooping cough started in the 1950s which led to a sharp fall in notifications. This decline was interrupted in 1974 following the publication of a number of case reports that were alleged to show that immunisation against whooping cough was linked to brain damage. The uptake of immunisation fell dramatically and large outbreaks of whooping cough followed in 1978 and 1982. In 1985 new evidence showed that immunisation was not the cause of brain damage and the uptake of immunisation increased again. The effect of this increase was that the expected four-yearly outbreak failed to happen for the first time in 1994.'

Source: Office for National Statistics, *Social Trends 28*, 1998

Table 4

Notifications of selected infectious diseases in the UK, 1971–96

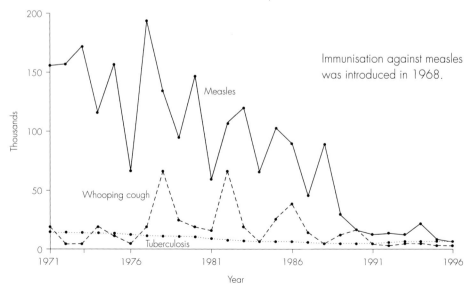

Source: PHLS Communicable Disease Surveillance Centre in *Social Trends 28*, 1998

Getting started

Outline the changes in the notifications of selected infectious diseases from Table 4. What pattern do you notice emerging?

Using the data in Table 2 and information about whooping cough given in Table 3, summarise the relationship between vaccinations and the outbreak of infectious diseases.

What sorts of precautions can be taken against food poisoning?

The report should include an outline of the trends in the notification of infectious diseases and consider the effects that non-vaccination has on these trends.

Going further

You will have noticed that there is no steady pattern in the data. It is obviously difficult to deal with fluctuating information. However, measures of central tendency can be identified in the data.

What is the mean number of notifications of infectious diseases for each of the diseases listed in Table 1?

The mean is calculated by the formula:

$$\frac{sum\ of\ observations}{number\ of\ observations}$$

In the case of tuberculosis, the mean number of reports in the period 1989–96 is:

$$\frac{6059 + 5897 + 6078 + 6441 + 6564 + 6228 + 6174 + 6238}{8} = 6210$$

to the nearest whole number.

For each disease, for how many years was the actual figure higher than the mean you have calculated? For how many years was it lower?

For which disease are the figures closest to the mean?

As there are variations from the mean, it might be better to calculate a three point moving average which will have the effect of smoothing out the data. For tuberculosis, the three point moving average is calculated by (a) finding the average for 1989–91, (b) finding the average for 1990–92, and so on. The calculations are as follows:

1989–91: $\dfrac{6059 + 5897 + 6078}{3}$ = 6011

1990–92: $\dfrac{5897 + 6078 + 6441}{3}$ = 6139

1991–93: $\dfrac{6078 + 6441 + 6564}{3}$ = 6361

1992–94: $\dfrac{6441 + 6564 + 6228}{3}$ = 6411

1993–95: $\dfrac{6564 + 6228 + 6174}{3}$ = 6322

1994–95: $\dfrac{6228 + 6174 + 6238}{3}$ = 6213

Remember, on your calculator you can find your first average and then multiply it by 3 to get back to the total, subtract 6059 and add 6441 and then divide by 3 to get the next average.

Calculate the three point moving average for each of the other diseases.

By estimating from Table 4, calculate a five point moving average for measles for the period 1971 to 1981.

What happens to the average notifications of measles between the periods 1971–81 and 1989–96? How does this reflect the success of the measles vaccination and the MMR vaccination over the period?

Drawing conclusions

Suggest what danger is involved for the general public and the health service in not taking public concerns about vaccinations seriously.

What options are open to the health service in terms of reassuring the public about health scares and vaccinations?

Should the MMR scare encourage a substantial number of parents not to vaccinate their children, the health service will need to respond. It could reassure the public that as the risk is minimal, the greater danger would be a loss of confidence and a trend similar to that which happened with whooping cough. Prepare a statement that might be issued putting forward this line of argument. Your statement should make use of the figures you have calculated.

Another policy might be to split the MMR vaccine into its individual parts. What would be the likely costs of this policy?

What sort of policy might be followed to reduce the incidence of food poisoning? Suggest a number of different solutions, outlining the advantages of each solution.

You might suggest, on the basis of a graph of your three point moving average for food poisoning, what the likely incidence of food poisoning will be by 2000.

As a business person, evaluate the proposition that more resources should be devoted to informing the public about the benefits of the MMR vaccine and public information on the handling of food.

Evaluating the data

What other information might you regard as useful for making a full analysis of the effects of a loss of public confidence in the MMR vaccine?

How useful is past information in attempting to plan for the future?

What problems would you encounter in attempting to monitor the effectiveness of policies designed to reduce the incidence of food poisoning?

Extension tasks

- To what extent is a loss of consumer confidence in a product of importance to a firm?
- What weapons does a firm have at its disposal to protect its name and reputation?
- Look out for press stories or television programmes which highlight problems people have in dealing with large companies. How effectively do you think that the firm deals with complaints?

How well did we do?

In this section you will:

- calculate the difference between budgeted and actual figures (i.e. the variance),
- understand the nature of the calculations,
- identify positive and negative variances and understand the difference between the two,
- suggest reasons and solutions for particular changes,
- appreciate the need for further information to be used in parallel with the variance analysis.

Your task

A business should always want to know what its forecasted sales figure look like, together with its forecasted profit, cash, wages etc. so that it can have some form of structure around which it can plan its decisions. Just as importantly, when a business gets to the end of a time period, it likes to ask 'How well did we do ?' Variance analysis is the process of comparing the actual performance of a business over a period of time with the forecasted or budgeted performance, making specific references to the differences and then going on to suggest reasons and possible solutions.

You are advising a company which manufactures ornamental money boxes for sale overseas. The company has drawn up a budget with the planned level of sales, output, an assumed selling price and with set costs of production.

Use the data below to establish the differences between planned and actual performance. What might explain this difference?

Datafile

The purpose of putting together a budget is to plan for the future; a business must plan for labour to be available (and to be paid at the going rate), for materials to be supplied, for fixed costs to be paid, fixed assets to be purchased, products to be sold and delivered on time, and so on.

	Budget
Sales volume	1000
Selling price	£20
Sales revenue	£20000
Labour costs	£10000
Material costs	£6000
Fixed costs	£3000
Profit	£1000

We assume that labour and materials are variable costs. Labour is £10 per unit and materials are £6 per unit. These figures will have been based on standard costs, i.e. an observed cost based on past information.

The above figures are planned for the month of August 1998. Here are the actual results for August.

	Actual
Sales volume	1100
Selling price	£17
Sales revenue	£18700
Labour costs	£10450
Material costs	£6820
Fixed costs	£2650
Profit	(£1220)

Despite the fact that we have sold more products, the budgeted profit of £1000 has become a loss of £1220. This needs to be analysed in more detail, so the next step is to calculate a variance.

Getting started

Calculate the differences in each item for the forecast and actual budget. Does the change lead to an increase or decrease in the profit?

To what extent is the increase in volume the reason for the changes? What would the budget have looked like if it had assumed a volume of 1100?

	BUDGET	ACTUAL	VARIANCE
Sales volume	1000	1100	100
Selling price	£20	£17	(£3)
Sales revenue	£20000	£18700	(£1300)
Labour costs	£10000	£10450	(£450)
Material costs	£6000	£6820	(£820)
Fixed costs	£3000	£2650	£350
Profit	£1000	(£1220)	(£2220)

You will notice that some figures are in brackets. A bracketed figure means that profit will be less as a result of the change (negative variance); a non-bracketed figure means that profit will be more (positive variance).

For this calculation we simply subtract budget from actual and then check whether the change increases or decreases profit. Look at the table's note to remind yourself of the reason for brackets.

Reasons for positive variance = sales higher or costs lower than expected (i.e. in the budget)
Reasons for negative variance = opposite of the above.

As a final check, the sum of all the variances of revenue and total costs should equal the difference between the budgeted profit and the actual profit. Always check this before going further.

Going further

We now look for reasons behind these changes. We begin by considering the nature of revenue and costs. If the volume has changed, it will affect both the revenue and variable costs. Revenue could change up or down depending on the price elasticity of demand for the product, but even if volume rises, so should variable costs (all other things being equal). We therefore remove the effect of volume by asking the following question:

What would the budget have looked like, had the company estimated the correct level of volume ?

What do you notice about revenue and costs? What might explain the differences?

The actual volume is 1100, so if
we repeat the budget with 1100
as the volume figure and no
other changes we get the
following answer:-

	FLEXED BUDGET	ACTUAL	FLEXED VARIANCE
Sales volume	1100	1100	0
Selling price	£20	£17	(£3)
Sales revenue	£22000	£18700	(£3300)
Labour costs	£11000	£10450	£550
Material costs	£6600	£6820	(£220)
Fixed costs	£3000	£2650	£350
Profit	£1400	(£1220)	(£2620)

You will note that fixed costs
stay the same in the flexed
budget as in the original. This
is because we are altering
volume – the definition of fixed
costs is that they do not change
with output.

This shows that had we estimated the volume correctly when we were drawing up the
original budget, the expected profit would have been £1400, making the variance even
higher at (£2620)! So the effect of the volume increase was actually to increase profit.
We calculate this change by comparing the variance with the flexed variance.

Variance	Flexed variance	The difference between these two figures is £500, i.e. once we adjust for the new volume, profit is £500 less; so the volume variance must be +£500 (because we have sold more than expected).
(£2120)	(£2620)	

Drawing conclusions

Having taken account of the volume change, we can now look at the flexed variance column again and see that the variance in the revenue column is (£3300). This must be entirely due to the price change, i.e. profit has fallen by £3300 due to the reduction in price.

This can be calculated by:

(actual price – budgeted price)   × actual volume
     (£17 – £20)   ×   1100   = (£3300).

We will discuss the reasons for this change later.

Next we move on to costs. If the change in the labour cost is £550, profit is £550 larger due to the usage of labour improving (an increase in productivity) and/or the cost of labour decreasing (through lower wage rates). The latter change is less likely, but unless more information is available we cannot conclude in any more detail.

The material costs have not improved in the same way. Indeed, they have increased by £220. Again, we can conclude that either the material cost per unit has increased (perhaps if the supplier simply raises prices) or that the raw material commodity price has increased on the market. Alternatively, the company could be less productive with materials; this could be explained either by the company attempting to increase quality, thereby using more materials per unit, or by the workforce wasting more materials.

The fixed cost variance of £350 could be explained by anything, although in the short run, output cannot be the culprit. Perhaps rates have fallen, or the company has had an electricity rebate, or interest rates have fallen.

Evaluating the data

The investigation above looks at particular causes of the difference between planned and actual budget outcomes. But what might lie behind the data? Remember that the links between cause and effect might be difficult to establish. What might, for example, lie behind the fall in price? How many different explanations can you think of?

> To look at only one change is good enough, but more thoughtful and deep analysis would link the changes observed with plausible reasons for the change. For example, the price has fallen by 15%, leading to an demand increase of 10%: the product is price inelastic and therefore the business should have <u>increased</u> the price. What has caused the price reduction? Perhaps an attempt to undercut the competition: the increase in demand will have forced output to increase and the workforce may have negotiated a bonus for the extra 10%. The bonus could have pushed them to work harder, and improved labour productivity (hence the positive labour cost variance). But this has meant that work has been rushed, and there has been more wastage.

> The above argument is not only plausible, but is substantiated by the figures. To summarise the variances we need to evaluate the overall effects: looking at each of the figures, we can see that by far the most significant reason for the reduction in profit is the reduction in the price, which reduced profit by £3300. Clearly the company was forced into this move, but it failed to produce the increase in volume necessary to increase either revenue or profit. This reveals the primary weakness of variance analysis, that it does not present the company with anything more than a quantitative summary of the difference between the budget and the actual. Apart from assuming that the budgeting procedure was accurate and well researched in the first place, we need more information to put the variances into their proper context.

Extension tasks

- Make a list of all the reasons why actual results might be different from budgeted figures for
  - (a) a manufacturer of oil-based chemicals, operating in America and Britain,
  - (b) a supermarket renowned for its high quality which, as part of its expansion plans, has just taken over a smaller rival which sells lower quality products.

Gibson Garage

In this section you will:

▶ calculate the unit cost of each item after allocating a proportion of the estimated fixed overheads (absorption costing).

Your task

Gibson Garage has three different departments: the paint shop; mechanical and servicing; and sales of components and spares. Tim Gibson, the owner, is concerned at the level of profit being made and has decided to consider each department as a separate cost centre, so that he can see where the profit comes from.

> As an independent financial adviser, write a report to Tim advising him as to whether he needs to restructure his business.

Datafile

Assume all costs and revenue are for 100% of the available floor space.

Table 1

Direct costs

Paint shop	£40 000 per year
Servicing/mechanical	£100 000 per year
Sales	£15 000 per year

Table 2

Indirect costs

General admininistration   £150 000 per year
Indirect costs are allocated according to the floor area taken up by each department:

paint shop		servicing/mechanical		sales
3	:	5	:	2

Table 3

Annual revenue

department	jobs per year	average price per job (£)
Paint shop	200	250
Servicing/mechanical	1000	200
Sales	5000	250

Table 4

Assume that all departments have sufficient work for expansion and that this would involve the same ratio 3: 5: 2 of both costs and revenue. For example, if the paint shop expanded into the sales area, then its revenue from the new area would be:

$$\frac{200}{10} \times 2 \times £250 = \frac{£10\,000}{\text{per year}} = \frac{\text{jobs per year}}{\text{total space}} \times \frac{\text{sales area}}{\text{space}} \times \frac{\text{average price}}{\text{per job}}$$

Its costs would be:

$$\text{direct costs} \quad = \frac{£40\,000}{10} \times 2 = \quad £8000$$

$$\text{indirect costs} = \frac{£150\,000}{10} \times 2 = £30\,000$$
$$\underline{} \; £38\,000 \;\; \text{TOTAL COSTS}$$

The garage could subcontract spray work to a local firm for £250 per job.

Getting started

Calculate the following:
- level of costs for all three areas (allocation of indirect costs),
- level of revenue for all three areas,
- profit levels.

From this you should be able to identify the 'weak' area(s) of the company and begin to consider which department would be the most profitable to expand.

Going further

It is often easiest to organise data in a table, so that it can be reviewed clearly:

	paint shop	servicing/mechanical	sales	total
Direct costs				
Indirect costs				
Total costs				
Revenue				
Profit				

You could use a spreadsheet to record these data. To allocate indirect costs:

$$\frac{\text{total indirect cost}}{\text{total floor area}} \times \text{floor area for each department}$$

e.g. for the sales department: $\dfrac{150\,000}{10} \times 2 = £30\,000$

To calculate revenue:

price × number of jobs.

To calculate profit:

total revenue – total costs.

Drawing conclusions

You should now be able to identify the 'weak' area(s) of the business. The next step is to consider Tim's option.

Is there anything which can be done to make the 'weak' department profitable?

This could involve cutting costs, i.e. efficiency improving measures of increasing total revenue.

Work out the price per job that each department needs to charge to break even, using the data given in Tables 1–3 and the following formula:

$$\text{break-even price per job} = \frac{\text{total cost}}{\text{output}}$$

This could then be compared to competitors' prices to draw a conclusion.

Can the business be restructured?

You would need to advise which department should expand and which should be removed. It would also be useful for you to show profit before and after the restructuring of the business, so that Tim could see clearly the benefits of the strategy.

Evaluating the data

> You now have enough information to write your report to Tim Gibson. Ensure that you explain clearly and support your conclusions, e.g. by quoting how much profit would increase if a certain department is expanded.

> Advise your client of any assumptions you have made in forming your conclusions, i.e. that there is plenty of business for expansion, and whether you need to undertake further research such as looking at the activities of competitors.

You have allocated the indirect costs by reviewing the floor space used by each department. Is this the most appropriate method for this type of activity?

Extension tasks

- Consider other methods, or criteria, for the allocation of indirect costs. How would your conclusions differ?
- Would Tim be better served focusing on a single department? What are the advantages and disadvantages of focusing on one line of business?

Skylark Ltd

Your task

Labour backbenchers, councillors and privately a few government ministers, have been raising the political temperature over the many advantages Scotland and Wales enjoy over the English regions – principally, their spending per head being 16% more than England's.

You work for Skylark Ltd which is considering relocating in the UK. Write a report to the Board evaluating which region of the UK is most appropriate.

Datafile

Table 1

Central government spending per head (£), 1994–95

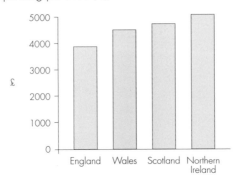

Table 2

Central government's block grants to the regions, 1997–98

Scottish Office   £14.3bn
Welsh Office   £6.9bn
Northern Ireland Office   £8.3bn

Table 3

Comparison of block grants, 1988/89 – 1995/96

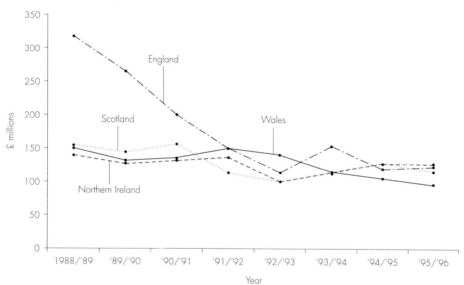

Table 4

Relative gross domestic product per head, 1995 (UK average = 100)

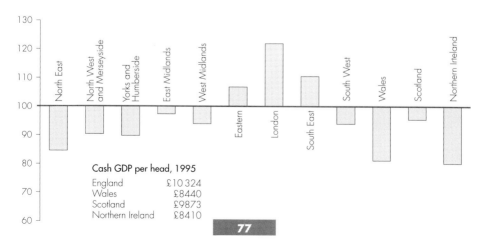

Cash GDP per head, 1995

England   £10 324
Wales   £8440
Scotland   £9873
Northern Ireland   £8410

| Table 5 |

The Barnett formula

'In 1976, a study of relative government spending was undertaken for Scotland, Wales and Northern Ireland. It showed a bias in favour of Scotland and Wales in terms of calculated need versus the actual money spent. As a result, in 1978 the Labour Treasury Chief Secretary, Joel (now Lord) Barnett, devised a formula under which 'block' funding from the Treasury would be calculated. The formula, revised slightly in 1992, is designed to ensure that Scottish and Welsh needs, then perceived to be greater than the average for Britain, were met, and is based on relative population, incidence of certain diseases and the cost of building roads in remote places.
- Under the Barnett formula, for every £85 change in the spending of relevant English departments with equivalents in Edinburgh and Cardiff (Education, Health, etc.), Scotland receives £10 and Wales £5.
- This currently means that when spending in equivalent departments in England and Wales is increased (or cut), the Scottish block grant gains (or loses) about 10 per cent of the change.
- The block grant for Northern Ireland is calculated according to an adaptation of the Barnett formula, which takes account of the greater security spending.'

Source (Tables 1–5): *Financial arrangements for UK devolution* by David Heald, Neal Geaughan, Colin Robb (University of Aberdeen)

| Table 6 |

Regional assistance to Northern Ireland

year	grant (£m)
1993	28 000
1994	33 600
1995	39 200

Getting started

Consult the glossary in your textbook for the definitions of any terms you are not sure of.

Investigate the difference between government spending per head in the different regions, using Tables 1–5.

Why is GDP per head important to Skylark's relocation plans?

What other grants do the regions receive? What has happened to these over time?

What are the implications of these changes in government grants to your location decision?

Going further

Check how the data in each table are presented. For example, the chart in Table 4 is expressed as index numbers, with 100 being the UK average, i.e. the 'base value' from which the other figures are calculated.

Index numbers are a convenient way of showing change in a set of data; however they say nothing about actual values. They do not say that London's GDP per head is £120, for example, but that it is 20% greater than the UK average.

Using Table 1, calculate the percentage difference between England and the other regions in terms of government expenditure per head.

The formula for this calculation is:

$$\frac{\text{English government expenditure per head} - \text{N. Ireland's government expenditure per head}}{\text{English government expenditure per head}} \times \frac{100}{1}$$

Consider the changes over time in government regional assistance, identifying trends (see Table 3).

For example, there was a steady decline in regional assistance to England during the period 1988–93, after which assistance has been on a level with the other regions.

Drawing conclusions

Your report may either consider each set of data in turn or concentrate on one side of the debate at a time, e.g. positive and negative effects for your relocation decision. Whichever approach you take, it is important that you integrate your results and focus on the task.

Consider the effect of each country's level of government assistance.

The data need to be applied; remember this is a debate on the relocation of a firm.

You will need to make judgements on what to include and what to leave out. You will also need to bring other points into the debate which are not in the data, e.g. other factors affecting the relocation decision, i.e. land price, availability of labour.

If there are contradictions in the data, acknowledge these in your report, rather than ignore them, as this may suggest you do not understand the data.

Evaluating the data

It is important that you address issues about the data. Table 3 expresses regional assistance (£ millions) over time, but does not take into account the impact of inflation. In order to do this, the real value of the grants needs to be considered.

A figure is in 'real terms' when its value has been adjusted for changes in the purchasing power of money. Normally, this is done by deflating by an appropriate index number of prices. The resulting value constitutes the real regional grant at constant prices.

This sounds very technical but, at the least, you need to acknowledge that prices will have risen over time so that the value of any grant will have diminished on a pound for pound basis, in terms of purchasing power.

Using Table 6, work out regional assistance to Northern Ireland in terms of index numbers.

If we make the base year 1993 and therefore make that value equal to 100, then the other values will be set relative to this:

1994: $\dfrac{33\,600}{28\,000} \times \dfrac{100}{1} = 120$

1995: $\dfrac{39\,200}{28\,000} \times \dfrac{100}{1} = 140$

As the table below shows, the benefits of indexing are that it makes trends understandable at a glance.

year	grant (1993 = 100)
1993	100
1994	120
1995	140

Extension task

- Evaluate the importance of government grants to a firm, e.g. geographical immobility.

Laura Ashley falls from grace

In this section you will:

► **consider the impact of bias upon data sources.**

Your task

On 15 January 1998, shares in the clothing and home-furnishings retailer Laura Ashley fell 25% to 26p, a new low, as the company gave warning that it was heading towards a £26m loss.

> As an investigative journalist, write an editorial comment for *The Retailer*, the industry's journal, outlining the reasons for and the implications of Laura Ashley's declining share price. Comment upon the policies being pursued by the company and suggest alternatives.

Datafile

Table 1

Laura Ashley grand design in tatters

Julia Finch

SHARES in fashion group Laura Ashley slumped to a record low yesterday as City experts speculated that the company was close to collapse.

The share price tumbled 20 per cent to 27.5p – compared to a peak of 219p less than two years ago – as the group unveiled another catalogue of disasters.

The retailer admitted to extremely poor Christmas sales, warned that its losses would be far greater than had been expected and announced that it was to sell off all its British manufacturing capacity.

Four factories in Wales – where the Ashley empire was founded in 1963 – and one in the Netherlands are to be sold, in a move that will affect nearly 700 staff.

The sewing operations in Oswestry and Gresford are being closed, as are the fabric and wallpaper printing operations in Newtown and Carno. They have a book value of £8.5 million.

Two other Laura Ashley factories in Wales were sold last year. John Taylor, chief executive of the Development Board for Rural Wales, said: "It's an opportunity for the new owners to - focus on manufacturing and build on the strengths and skills of the workforce."

Lord Hooson, the Liberal peer and former Laura Ashley chairman, said: "I happen to disagree with some of the decisions taken recently but I think there's a very good future for the factories if they are properly managed."

A company spokesman claimed £70 million worth of new loans guaranteed survival at least to spring 1999.

Laura Ashley, whose stock-in-trade was a fashion innovation in the 1970s, has been brought to its knees in little over two years by the ambitious expansion strategy pursued by its former chief executive, Ann Iverson, who departed with a £450 000 pay-off in November.

An American retailer brought in to revitalise the British brand, Ms Iverson changed the company's fashion style and aimed for aggressive expansion in the US.

The Laura Ashley company, which was worth more than £500 million only 18 months ago, now has a stockmarket valuation of little more than £60 million. Yesterday they said it was going back to its roots, retrenching in the US and shutting down its factories in order to survive.

Slow sales, serious over-stocking and a need to improve cash flow forced the company to start its winter sale well ahead of the festive season. But yesterday Laura Ashley revealed that sales were

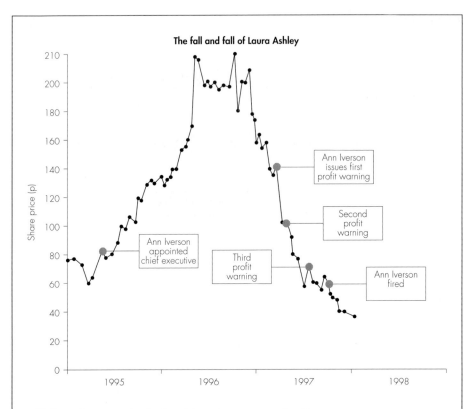

The fall and fall of Laura Ashley

Share price (p)

Ann Iverson issues first profit warning

Second profit warning

Ann Iverson appointed chief executive

Third profit warning

Ann Iverson fired

1995　1996　1997　1998

still down 3 per cent in the last 24 weeks – or 8 per cent including the effect of the strong pound.

US sales have dipped by 13 per cent in seven weeks. The company admitted: "Trading has been particularly difficult in North America."

David Hoare, the management consultant drafted in to dig the company out of its hole, has appointed Michael Appel, a specialist retailing trouble-shooter, to its US business. A spokesman said: "His primary task is to stabilise the business".

The company warned investors that its problems would mean a loss of £23 million – £26 million for the full year – nearly three times the level analysts were expecting only a few months ago and £10 million more than the firm's own brokers

were estimating.

The loss does not include restructuring costs. Yesterday the company refused to comment on the scale of these charges, but it is understood they could be in the region of £10 million.

In an attempt to update its trademark fashion look, a new designer has been installed with a brief to "re-identify Laura Ashley".

But City analysts are not convinced that the company can make a comeback. Roy Maconochie of Henderson Crosthwaite said: "They cannot make a go of it without major downsizing, and only a liquidator could afford it."

Another analyst said: "There is a brand worth salvaging but the debts are mounting up."

Both questioned whether the banks would stand by the company.

Source: *Guardian*, 16 January 1998

Table 2

Laura Ashley shares dive to record low

By Kate Rankine, City Correspondent

THE CRISIS at Laura Ashley deepened yesterday when the troubled clothing and home furnishings company warned of escalating losses, particularly in America, and said it plans to sell its Welsh manufacturing business.

Shares in Laura Ashley yesterday plunged $8^1/_2$ to 26p, the lowest ever in its 13-year history as a public company, after the group said it would lose between £23m and £26m for the year ending January.

After making undisclosed restructuring charges, the loss will be even greater. Only this time last year, analysts were forecasting Laura Ashley would make up to £24m pre-tax profit for the current financial year.

Yesterday's severe profit warning is the fourth since last April and even shocked the company's own stockbrokers, Dresdner Kleinwort Benson, which only two months ago predicted it would lose £15m before tax.

One analyst said yesterday: "It is an extraordinary situation. It is a matter of urgency that they tackle the American business. Unless the management closes the US business or put it into Chapter 11, the whole thing is going under. They have got to find some more cash from somewhere."

Last month, Laura Ashley managed to persuade its banks to extend their committed borrowing facilities, totalling £70m, until April next year after the company had breached at least one of its banking covenants.

But, because of the precarious nature of its finances, Laura Ashley must meet its bankers at the end of every month in order to review its banking covenants.

David Hoare, the company's chief executive who replaced Ann Iverson last November, met the company's banks on Wednesday evening to inform them of the predicted losses and a disastrous Christmas.

Sales in America, excluding the impact of foreign exchange, plunged by 13pc during the seven weeks to January 10 and the new US stores performed appallingly. These new American stores are the legacy of Mrs Iverson's two-year reign when the company opened 32 large stores in the US, concentrating on selling home furnishings. The leases were signed for 10 years and analysts believe the losses at these stores are escalating.

Laura Ashley yesterday appointed American Michael Appel, 48, whom it described as a turnaround specialist, on a six-month contract as chief executive of its North American business.

He will be helped by management consultants, Parthenon, and Olivier Roux, the French-born management consultant who was the star witness in the Guinness trial eight years ago. Mr Hoare said he hoped a recovery plan will be announced before the results are disclosed on April 23.

"We are developing a recovery plan for the business at the moment. A full range of options are being considered," he said.

Mr Hoare said it was a unanimous decision to put its Welsh and Dutch factories up for sale.

Sir Bernard Ashley, the husband of the late Laura and who owns 35pc of the company, is considering making an offer for at least one of the Welsh factories.

US investment bank Goldman Sachs, where Laura Ashley's chairman John Thornton is on the six-man executive committee, is handling the sale.

Source: *Daily Telegraph*, 16 January 1998

Getting started

Read the two newspaper articles shown in Tables 1 and 2.

> *What you need to be aware of is that the priority/bias is different in the two articles.*

Going further

List (a) the reasons, (b) the implications, and (c) the policies as identified in each article.

> *When selecting material for your report, ensure that it is supported by quoting statistics or using text quotes.*

Drawing conclusions

From each article place into rank order the reasons given for the decline of Laura Ashley.

> *You could use a table format.*

The material may reveal contradictions. Using the graph given in Table 1, what conclusions would the company have drawn about the former chief executive's performance (a) in mid-1996, (b) in early 1997, and (c) in mid-1997? Why might this be the case?

Can you conclude from the graph whether the former chief executive was central to the decline in Laura Ashley's fortunes?

> *Outline the implications stated and try to prioritise these. For example the Guardian article discusses job losses resulting from factory closures, whereas the Daily Telegraph comments on plans to sell Laura Ashley's Welsh manufacturing business.*

Consider the policy options suggested. Are they appropriate? Do they address the problems?

Evaluating the data

You should now have enough information to write your article.

Ensure your conclusions are supported. You will need to consider the issues concerning where this material has come from so that you may counterbalance any bias, e.g. the political sympathies of the paper, who was interviewed, whether the information was up-to-date, when the information was selected. Refer back to the graph in Table 1 and the different perceptions of company performance at different times.

Extension tasks

- What other information do you require before writing your article?
- How would Laura Ashley's press statement differ from the newspaper articles? Why?
- Why do firms 'window dress' their results or statements to the public?